Ten in the Den

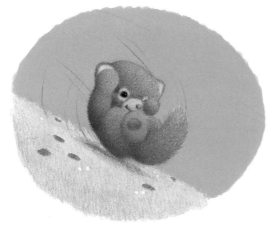

For Joshua James
J. B.

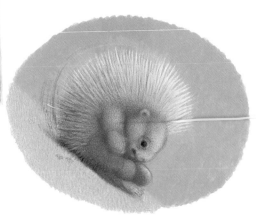

www.johnbutlerart.com

ORCHARD BOOKS
96 Leonard Street, London EC2A 4XD
Orchard Books Australia
32/45-51 Huntley Street, Alexandria NSW 2015
ISBN 1 84362 650 0
First published in Great Britain in 2005
Text and illustrations © John Butler 2005

Ten in the Den

John Butler

ORCHARD BOOKS

There were **ten** in the den,
and the little mouse said,

"Roll over! Roll over!"
So they all rolled over and . . .

. . . Rabbit fell out.

Floppetty,

hoppetty,

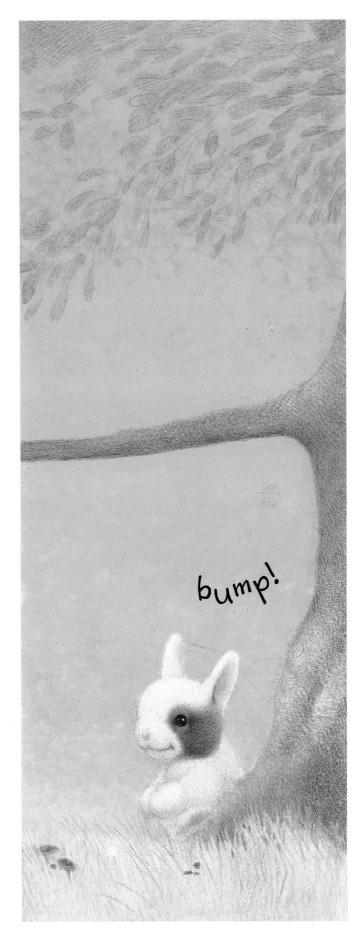

bump!

There were **nine** in the den,
and the little mouse said,

"Roll over! Roll over!"
So they all rolled over and . . .

. . . Mole fell out.

Roly,

poly,

bump!

There were **eight** in the den,
and the little mouse said,

Slippy,

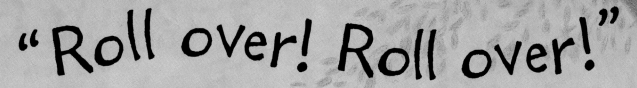

"Roll over! Roll over!"
So they all rolled over
and Beaver fell out.

slidey,

bump!

There were **seven** in the den,
and the little mouse said,

"Roll over!
Roll over!"

So they all rolled over and . . .

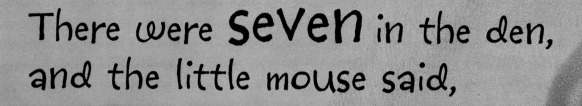

. . . Badger fell out.

Bouncy, pouncy,

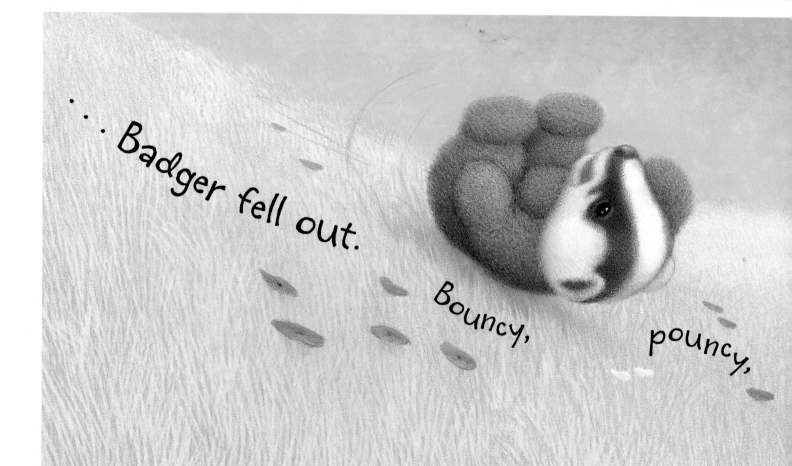

bump!

There were **SIX** in the den,
and the little mouse said,

"Roll over! Roll over!"
So they all rolled over and . . .

...Porcupine fell out.

Prickly,

tickly,

bump!

There were **five** in the den,
and the little mouse said,

"Roll over! Roll over!"
So they all rolled over and . . .

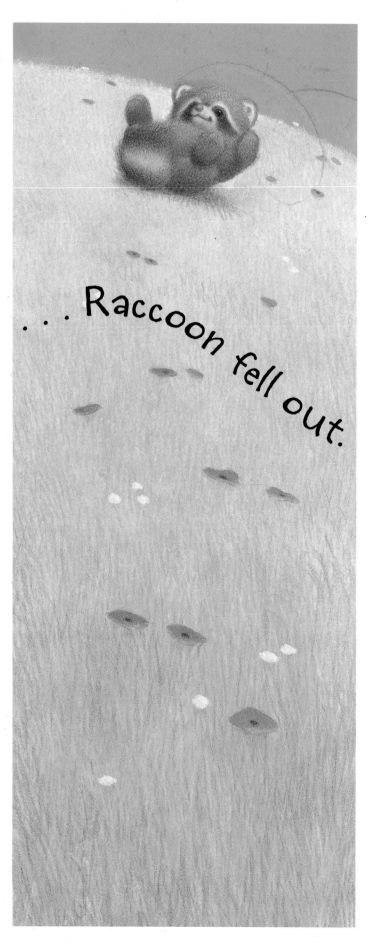

. . . Raccoon fell out.

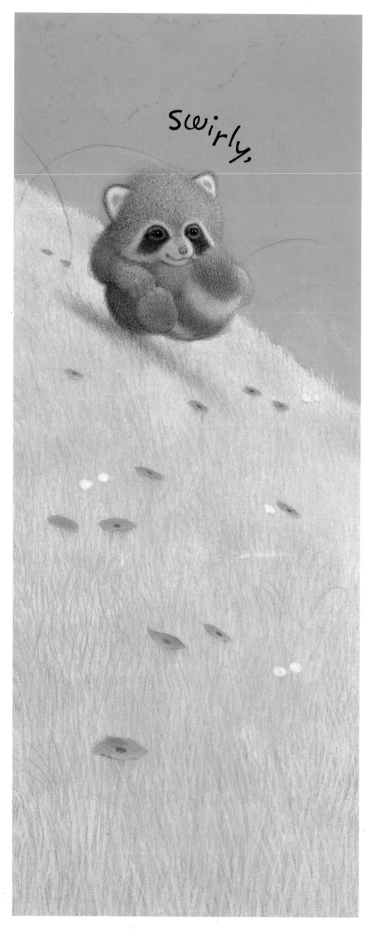

Swirly,

There were **four** in the den,
and the little mouse said,

"Roll over! Roll over!"
So they all rolled over and . . .

. . . Fox fell out.

Rumbly,

tumbly,

bump!

There were **three** in the den,
and the little mouse said,

"Roll over! Roll over!"

So they all rolled over
and Squirrel fell out.

squiggly,

wiggly,

bump!

. . . Bear fell out.

Bumpety, thumpety,

There were **two** in the den,
and the little mouse said,

"Roll over!
Roll over!"

So they both rolled over and . . .

bump!

There was **one** in the den,
and the little mouse sniffed,

"I miss my friends!"

So he rolled over and scampered out.

"Wait

for

me!"

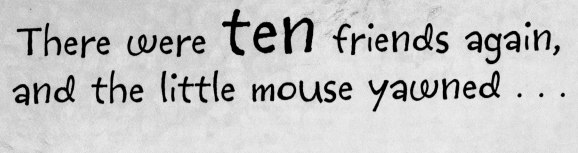

There were **ten** friends again,
and the little mouse yawned . . .

"Night night,
sleep tight!"

So they all snuggled together and . . .

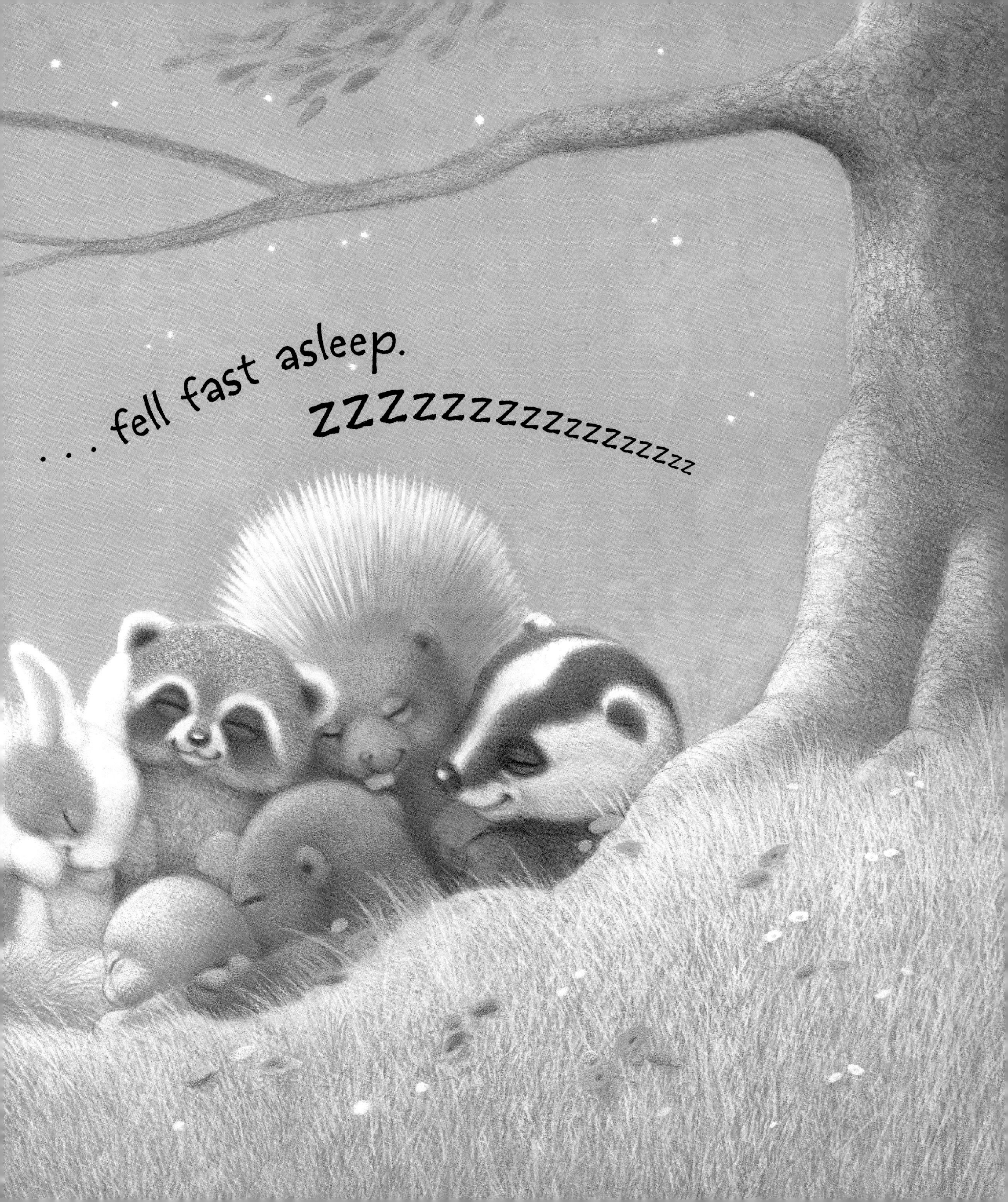

. . . fell fast asleep.

zzzzzzzzzzzzzzzzz

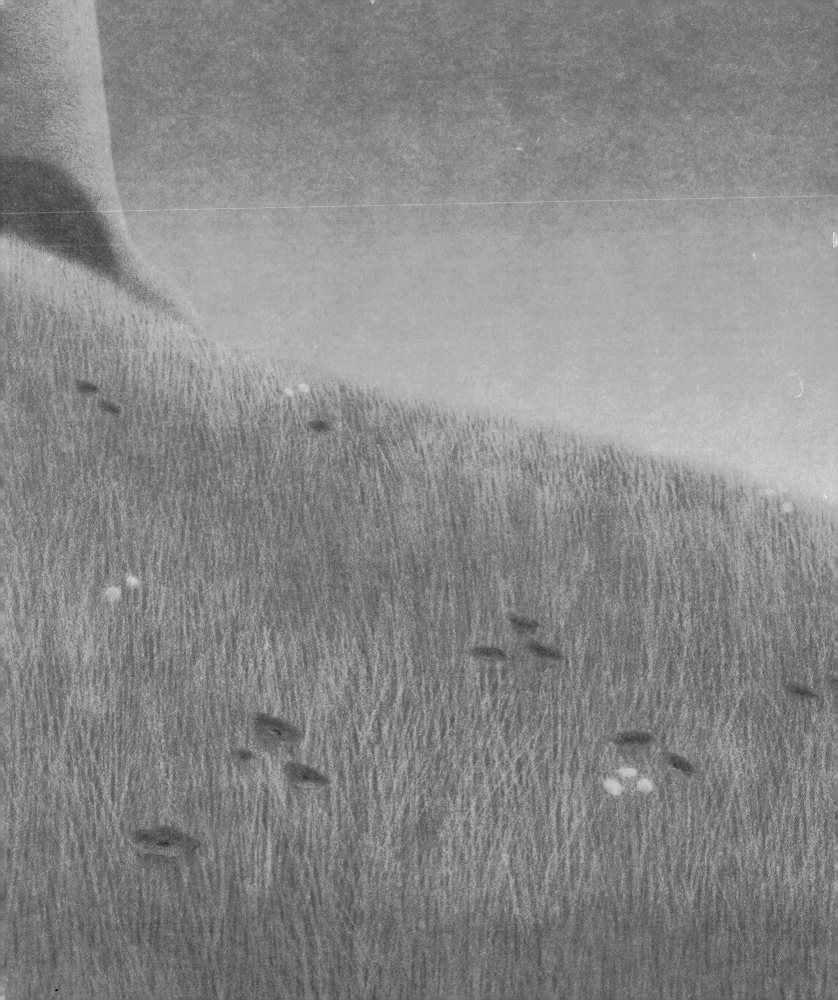